To John Ciardi

mathew Tenson

BELIEF
OF THE
STRANGER

BELIEF
OF THE
STRANGER

BY

Mathew Tenon

A. S. Barnes and Company
South Brunswick and New York
Thomas Yoseloff Ltd, *London*

© 1961, 1968 by A. S. Barnes and Company, Inc.

Library of Congress Catalogue Card Number:
68-29865

A. S. Barnes and Co., Inc.
Cranbury, New Jersey 08512

Thomas Yoseloff Ltd
18 Charing Cross Road
London WC 2, England

6957
Printed in the United States of America

CONTENTS

I

CONSUMMATIONS AND FIDELITIES
Psalmic Odes

II

A NEARNESS

III

THE HOUSE OF THE BELOVED

I

CONSUMMATIONS AND FIDELITIES
Psalmic Odes

FIRST ODE

In the midst of all my
Getting and my doing comes
Something into me that cares not
Of the getting and the doing.
A calm, an equipoise that
Has its own gentle consonance,
Existing without struggle or violence,
Preserving a floating hub
In the wheel of things.
It comes and I feel it.
Yet I cannot grasp or touch
It more than I can touch the sunlight.
It touches me, and I am content.

SECOND ODE

Now I begin to feel the sun of understanding,
How it glows and pales and wakens me.
It opens me and fills my darkness.
It makes me to roll up my lashes
And put away sleeping angers and idles.
The beams danced before me day after
Day and I stirred not.
Now I unfold to them
And strive to know.
They filter into a hungering
Mind where once they beat upon skin.
My eyes were glazed against them and were
Only for the steps of the treadmill.
The distance from step to step
Is small and narrow
But the measures from pillar to pillar
In the fields of wisdom are many times great
And are not filled with feet.
The colors of life live in this sun.
They play and work upon my earth
And bring forth many
Flowers before the slow fruit.
The treadmill turns still but it has

Ceased in my thoughts,
For my thoughts have come out
Of the churning.
I shall delight in my time
And keep a bright watch.

THIRD ODE

May the love mystical and kind
Increase in me this day.
May it rise up and run into
The blood of my nature
Like a precious liquor.
May it run among my thoughts
And find understanding.
May it spill my measure
And make a sweet smell in my fire.
How delightful are the signs
And essences.
The world about me is altered,
The time of the day is made good
And a way is cleared
In the confusion.
My fire flickers, yet
The subtle aroma wakens me.
It makes me stronger than my limbs,
It makes me supple as the glove
And to take rich comfort in what can be.
I shall cherish it and breathe its names.

FOURTH ODE

I arise from cool slumbers
To go and set my sail upon
The untrod water.
What little reckoning I hold
Will serve as compass well enough.
My sinews are tender yet I trust
Them more than a mooring of precious
Metal for they grow with trial.
If no breeze waits for me at the door
I shall go and find one to set
My blade across.
The rise and fall
Of the swell gives pleasure.
It rocks me and plays into my
Thoughts and being with its travel.
My blood responds and my
Cells keep the time of their life
And the time and beat messaged to them.
Perhaps I shall catch
One or two of the lines that reflect
In the trackless waters.
They sometimes show themselves through
The watery clarity.

I shall take them up deftly
As reins upon a gentle sea horse
And sense their traces
Among the currents.
My sail is as myself,
No better, no worse.
Free to raise at will,
Supple to lighten and furl,
Worn as expected,
Many times soiled
And many times sun-washed and whitened.
This day I go without a friend,
All will be secret friend to me.
They are as the elusive
Fishes of the water
And the birds of the air.
Some swooping to look at me,
Some veering off, some fearful.
Some laughing at me, I laughing in return.
Many more beautifully
Marked and smoother.
All seeming molded and made
For their element better than I.
But my element extends
Beyond vision and I shall fit it well.
Some are mean of looks and large,
Others are deer-eyed.
All glide by hardly looking my way.

I take from them all and give to them all.
Some feel they would tear me into
Pieces and devour me,
But they see their teeth
Do not find me.
Others would bring good things
And cast them near
As near their young,
But I am not wanting.
These are the poles
The startling extremes
And I perceive that it is
A mistake to believe the main
Is made with them.
The multitude would
Have but a look hurriedly taken
And go their way,
While I continue my course,
Being fully alive and of good cheer
And bobbing a bit of colour over the deep.
So the great body of human
Fishes and birds go about their
Matters with a busy, nodding
And sometimes sulky acquaintance.
And my craft sails on
Hailing them and wishing them well,
And finding harbour in many strange places.

FIFTH ODE

The hours cease and I ponder them.
What came of them? Where is my gain?
And yet, why weigh time so?
Do I live in my pockets?
Have I forgotten the get of life is never enough?
Or perhaps the spell of the get and count
Has stilled my senses.
It is a donkey plod and my being has
Fallen asleep on little feet.
Fitness sets the world turning and this is
The motion to rouse in
The stride and love of life,
Catching up life itself for its own sake,
For the strange winding and unwinding of it,
Curiously stumbling into hidden dramas
Of ants and men tugging
On the stems and ropes of things.
Not for acceptance but wonder,
Not for closures
But openings,
Nor for thin speed
But for the life of dimensions.
Life that walks off the burning

Highway of get and get and get
And pauses to look around,
Finding there is no need to burn intensity
When there is awareness,
Noticing how the sight of awareness is
As a stream of silver arrows touching
The shades and uttermost tips of things.
Yes, I shall go now and stretch my being,
Striding out on the avenues
With a light and easy sway.
My existence seems to flare
And extend beyond me.
I pause and look about
Casting my senses over the expanse,
Spending and wasting time by a new clock.
Then move slowly on,
Gently cracking the shells of experience.

SIXTH ODE

Let me go now and search among
The strange and beautiful faces
For I would be lost a while and mingled.
Down the avenue down from Alberta wheatfields
And the air of meadowlarks striding limber
And easy a manly fellow of broad open face
Full-meeting my eyes, well nourished
And fit in fresh laundered clothes. High noon
Shines through his sandy cropped hair, a man
Not confused or scattered in pieces but whole.
A woman who walks in lillies of the moon
Approaches, distant dulcet of hollowing cheeks
A fine white powder suspended in her gaze.
How strangely beautiful to see
Her moving with her companion a spare man
Tall in a hard body that shines the patina
Of light rubbed leather, the reined cords
Of his neck drawn taut his cheeks
Burnished in the sun like Persian shields.
Behind them in fast tack a clicking stepper
Of San Juan style scattering a trail of music
And glances through the platinum pale
Of the girl from Sweden as she questions

Herself and her snow-ringed hours
Where frail archers of light
Shoot into drifts of lemon green mist.
Now comes a massive red nose over
A voice of barnacled wet rocks, short arms
Threshing and baggy legs quick stumping.
There a young fellow who must feed
On cactus thorn and lizards' tails and yet
Hearing says there is a brilliant tenderness
Behind the smooth hair and high cut nostrils.
No sooner gone than a face of white wine
Turning away in a faint smile of silver veils
And grey evening. The air of sylphs
Is not so rare, she moves yet waits in it.
Soon overtaking, a polished Nubian brow
Clusters of dewy grapes glistening in the pores
Perfect teeth flashing the sun of him
His biceps sheathed in ebony and frost, and all
The gentleness of clean power fluently moving,
Yet wild horses have left
A dying thunder in his look.
Now comes an invisible face never showing
A flicker of the marked intelligence within,
A hundred guesses will not catch
The train in her thought for it goes
On disappearing tracks.
Now a bloating face of alcohol lumps of starch
And malted eyes drowsing under neon lids

All propped up on nine teeth passing out
The starts of apologies.
Here come a pair of filling eyes
Swimming and laughing with some quirked
Story that lifts thin time up
And makes it plump.
Here a face of charted success that looks
Long at figures and never wanders from
What is right ahead, handsome clothed in grey
Red on weekends. In close behind a girl
Of eager-mouthed expectation, dart eyes
Hair placed forever,
The very nose of anxious confidence set
On a certain trail.
A surf of frothing green breaks
In this woman's jasper eyes beached in fair
Complexion well sanded with tiny strawberries
Her coral ears laid back tight
And seeming not to hear.
Angel fish have lost their
Way in these eyes among swift glances
And spears of black steel damascened in gold,
The easy curling lips drop soft accents
And honeysuckles; poppies and oranges play
In her brow netted and swept
By streams of rich dark hair.
And here at the corner a sudden girl
Freckled with wild rice, her long arms

Overflown with chestnut hair as they
Talk and jerk in articulate angles.
Carefully edging along the windows a walking
Parchment of intense study and precision,
His hair a close-hugging brown moss
A knot of wood spreading in one cheek
Diamond eyes that seem to crack
The glass they look in.
Here is a face woven of old baskets leaking
Weary looks, fingers wondering and wondering
Over the chin loose lips sucking and pushing,
Perhaps soon to be tended by this bold
Nurse of abrupt straight eyes and strong legs
Wide-striding in white shoes pointed out.
There cheekbones that could be Shawnee
Or Sioux or out of earliest times.
The large mouth firmly drawn from
A drum stretched over centuries of sundowns
Rain and fire a triangular jaw hammered
Out of fish scales and buffalo.
Slipping through them all the jag-toothed
Grin of a taunter escaped from school,
A punch of one act plays
And heavy-curtained frowns,
A whirl of yellow jasmin has caught his arm
And he's off in both directions.
Here passes a face of stained glass
Mottling reds and grey leaded panes enduring

And untouched in high stoned air.
And here is one of pox and fried creases smiling
Loyally with buck teeth and rusty wire eyebrows.
And here walks the plainest of the plain
Speaking wordlessly of a quiet home
Timid love and faithfulness,
A cloud of amethyst floating in her eyelashes.
Now one of sulk and brooding, coal mines sunk
Deep in her eyes and crushed rubies
Smoking on her lips.
The slender African antelope girl has the neck
Of a silver ewer, her lightly parted lips
Glow softly like Minoan sealstones.
Long bronze forks of her brother's
Keen glances reach far down the block
As he glides by, his body showing a frame
Of delicate bone in fine clear line.
Here close a little girl of new ivory with her
Mother of old ivory and rosewood eyes
Slow-paced in a painful gait, her throat
Puffing and clucking all the while.
From Hawaii a richly fleshed woman of carnelian
Tints dusted over with the mocha
Of butterfly wings, her large rounded chin
Blooming in cinnamon and almonds.
And there a crumpled paper bag face, slow eyes
Squeezing and squinting out of two
Small openings, a map of troubles

Perhaps never traveled.
Here is a bright brick face that might have
Lived off Galway Bay, the blue marble gaze
Staring out over a sea of sentiment surging
And rippling among friends loves and rivals.
Now a short fellow of melancholy eyes down
In old hammocks, a maze of little blood vines
And webs in his cheeks
A mouth escaping in a crippled dancer's twist.
And there swept along in a tango of olives
And powdered medallions a bitter mouth
Sensitive nostrils sharp shoulder blades
And patent leather eyes that dare.
There bobs a bouncing ball of a boy's head
Full of jiggling question marks
Mock challenge and shrill calls.
The unhurried exquisitely sinuous hand
There pointing in the window could be
Argentine or Malay or Italian, or is it
A newer blend? Now he deftly touches
The necklace round an alabaster
Neck more lovely than white,
The air about the momentary still seems
Crystalline and shimmering with roses and limes.
Looking on, the featureless clouded face
Of a young girl seeming already
Silenced and resigned, yet is it so?
At the last crossway a fierce

Deep-hacked face saying knowing encouraging
Words to an old woman, starting prickles
In her withered eyes
Proving the easy guesses wrong again.
And yet among all these many
I left not a spark.

SEVENTH ODE

I cry out to our sacred
Love to take up
The anguish within me.
To give heed and enter
My clots and ferment.
I cry out without words
From the depths of me.
Surely this love will
Take a share of my grief.
Surely it will lift
With its strong easing fingers
And comfort my bitterness.
Let it come now and suffuse my being.
Let it moisten my hide
And send drink to the fibers
Of my strength and my courage.
I bend down yet out of this
Shall I be nourished and drawn up
To greater measure as the fertile
Field beats down yet
Takes drink under the storm.
And the morning shall be new,
The rain shall sweep away.

EIGHTH ODE

Our love beareth flowers each day,
Of dark purpling reds
Of happiest yellows, of clear-eyed
Blues, and of a white serene.
And each day we give these
Flowers carelessly, in rich profusion,
Over the heave and breadth
Of the day, to the towering
And to the least, to the loving
And to those empty of love,
Expecting no return,
Hoping to be left with few to fade
And waste their scent and seed.

NINTH ODE

Look, look, my eyes, round yourselves.
Large and new-waked set this
A watching time as stepping aside
From my self I come alive in you and tear
The pale curtain from the play
Of life in this very act in which I stand.
Freed from what it means
To me, catching cues and hints
Of what it is to those who scamper
And totter across the earthy stage
We peer and listen
Taking life from life itself.
These are games comedies dramas
And momentary mimes done by
The only perfect actors performing
Not a remembered art but the little
Acts and lines that show the palm of life.
Now untied reality ravels out its fresh-writ
Script as it goes before.
Colors seem to change their keys
And even common street greys are
Seen shaded from immense palettes
Of pearl smoke silver and steel.

Gazing into the life of sudden instants
Men and women before half-seen as
Cardboard figures along my course
Now begin to round, seeming larger
And wondrous strange with their own
Story strands weaving, crossing and recrossing.
Now none goes unheeded and none is
Trimmed to acquaintance
Aid or thorn.
All judgments are suspended,
It is the time to see not to act,
To question not to answer,
To feel the human current
Not to sail it, to send balloons
Of wonder up above the crimson arrows.
And when my vision jades and clouds
With shadows of myself
I again step sidewards and hold up
An imaginary frame to part a single scene,
Dividing it crisply
Into special instants,
Looking for the particular,
Letting the threads of unity
Wait for another time.
The moments come forward in the watching-frame,
Cut from the steady troop and train of hours,
Snipped from the ties that held them
In old bundles, lifted from

The dull background made
Of single-tracking habits.
Moments too true and oddly ordinary
To be told in tales,
Feelings that were never named,
Pungent flashes that are quenched
Dried and flattened when preserved.
Alive, one scene teems a book
Of storied cause and meaning
Masked, unmasked and demi-masked.
I ask whence comes this stance, this flicker
That swallowed word, that rhythmed nod.
What is a quarter part of the meaning
Of that hand movement,
Who swims behind those eyes,
What is the old cause of this smile now?
Looking deeply, the bone that castles the mind
Is seen, the wish that turns the act,
The shadowed rest that rounds her moon.
Yes there is everywhere to see
Worlds that never meet the traveler's eye.
Though I did sightsee the cities yet until
I caught a sight of men and women I was
Home in bed for they have more streets
And byways than the globe can carry on its back.
Time will tell the observer
To others time is mum.

TENTH ODE

Through years of the days and days
I in my parts went by the high laws.
My voice sounded in good keys
And was fair with its words. And I
Lived according to right ways
And did my share and my measure,
And it was more than the giving
Of pats and gifts.
There were few who found
Fault in my ways or my words
For I ordered myself
And commanded myself to pass.
The nags of conduct I appeased and I
Escaped much trouble, but there was
No more, for the life was ruled bare
And gave no juice.
Then I turned about
And came to do such things
Not so much for the following as
The creation that comes of them
And rises distantly,
Beyond the hour and the day,
Sometimes appearing unnoticed

In a life close to mine
Or in my own, or perhaps
Touching those I would never know,
Or heard in the new brood of a warbler
Far off, even after my death.
I kept no watch nor
Wait for their produce
And came to be content for them
To work unseen and imperfectly,
Often falling by the way when
Hardly commenced. And then there came
Happiness in these things.

ELEVENTH ODE

My love left me in the cold night
And I was chilled and sick at heart.
Like the breath of caves
Loneliness came over me.
My time had stopped.
And the dampness
Of earth entered me as into one buried.
But then a far off flickering fire
Crept into my eyes.
Then another and another came up,
Along the road, beyond the dim hill, as far
As vision could reach, strewn carelessly
As from a vast sweeping arm.
I looked long in silence and sadness,
Hardly knowing light or dark
Or their parting.
And then I guessed they were
The scattered fires of love.
And I saw they were growing larger.
Larger and brighter and yet
More red, making islands in the black
Sky to move and blush.
The flames waxed and grew and rose up

In tumultuous towers until the islands ran
Together and all the sky was blood red
And streaked and the air about me was warmed.
Then it was crimson and bellied with swirling
Streams of yellow and thick grey until the earth
And the air above became a soundless inferno.
The roofs of houses shone and glistened brightly
And the tops of trees swayed and hurled
To and fro like flames on shifting winds
And they became not red but
Writhing green and grew taller.
Water ran down their trunks in silver
Torrents like sliding films of ice
Yet the leaves were dry.
Swallows flew up out of their roosts
And circled and hovered with strange ease
Their eyes becoming soft and large.
The sky could become no more red and was
Nearing bruised purple and black.
Suddenly white sheets of rain fell into
The inferno as though they were nothing.
Then there was a cooling and a gentle trembling
Rain prevailed and after a time it abated.
And then the high spirit swept through
Me and commanded me to take my
Little coal of love and make it many.
To take it that was narrow and make
It vast and kindly.

Then I saw that the inferno
Was gone away and it was peaceful.
And the little fires came up timidly again
One by one and comforted me.
I saw that my skin was not
Scorched but moist. And my heart was
Swelled and my vision was cloud-chased.
I said I will take my love in little
Twigs and cast them into the struggling fires.
I will plant embers where there are none.

TWELFTH ODE

Take my home, my flagged steps
And my favorite chair
The sun-drinking window on the open road
My hemlock and my yellow cat,
Take them, they are more than I can carry.
Yes the antique table for my
Tobacco and books, the nearness of friends
The old fashioned cups that talk
To one who lives alone,
Take them, so long as I may
Keep a bright hail for experience.

THIRTEENTH ODE

My heart shall grow large
Large as a melon of the vine fresh cut
That spilleth a little.
Full and shining with seed and juice
For I would not have it a puckered
Lemon drying in my cabinet.
Large with greening hopes and fresh remembrances,
With passing slights and chills that freeze
The air to a skyless bullring, with flying
Hooves dark lashes and lustrous eyes,
With blazed angers and smouldering wantings
And ashen fear. With the pale girl in her
Hospital bed and her slow-sinking eyes,
The full contralto voice as it climbs
Above the whiteness of the bride and her
Mate standing still and close.
The little child who peeped in my
Face and was carried away,
With entwining thoughts spun along the sidewalk
Traceless as a puff of dust,
The delicious aroma of burning leaves,
Curious glances from park benches,
The fleshy moulds of passing beauty,

The intent faces of lovers carefully
Unwrapping solitary words.
With the potent heavy-laden
Shelves of books in the richly carved library
And the cool new library shaped only
Of angles and light.
Out of the aura that streams from admired
Men and women, and the fiber and tenacity
Of an unbreakable one fighting a losing battle.
With the blood-soaked newspapers telling
Of war begetting war and the sullen
Disgust for the promotion of violence.
From the relentless press of eyes through
The cage of the passing prison van,
And the sparks off the teeth of the one who
Has no secret names for death.
The laughing jeer of the tenement
Woman who knows well enough,
Her red puffed ankles edging over the curb.
With the shy flicker of friendliness hovering
In the look of the stranger,
With the shine of the dark suit carefully
Pressed again, and the ebb and flow of a dress
On a well formed figure. With the supple play
Of young bodies on the winnowing sand,
The caress of the sea's foaming fingers
About my feet and the kiss of the breeze
On the back of my neck.

The pure clarity of fresh swept air from
The north and the west, the miraculous fires
Of the sinking sun, the return homeward
Past windows gleaming in the dusk.
With the robin's low call over the shadowed lawn
And the calm power of the darkening pines,
With the mysteriously gathering
Veil enfolding murmuring faces, with linen
Visions and soft repose.
The last payment of rent and the troubled
Move from home,
The dusty floors of empty rooms
And the cramping squeeze of shrinking scope.
With the shudder and then the slow
Pervasive burning, the sudden contempt for old
Comforts and the longing for motion
And fitness. The eagerness to take on
Whatever comes, the outward-curving sweep
Of the open road. The effuse and surge
Of confidence over all doubts.
The passage through the rich green divide
Breathing sun-warmed glades of laurel and grass
As I go between,
The stop unobserved near
The family at the picnic table
Watching the spread of food being layed out
And the bend of the mother over
The cooing infant.

With the defiant face of the boy marched
To his father, the vague answers
To simple questions. The lingering start onward
And the arrival so welcome at the farm
Splattered over the floor of the valley.
With the burst of full-risen morning sun
And patches of bright laughter,
The distant yelps of dogs,
The song and hum of the young housewife
At work in the kitchen,
The child's wail of burned fingers
And the swift scold. The clearness and good
Health of the spinster standing
In her garden far from the main road,
The fragrant lake of cool air
At the edge of the wood, the plump
Hollow gurgle of the brook beneath
Dripping banks. Out of bits of me
Clinging to a black twig as it winds
And twists in the orb of the pool,
The glittering eyes of the schoolgirl
Surprised at her desk,
The scent of warm lilac drifting
Over the windowsill. The memory of empty letters,
The whispering depths of loneliness, the pause
Beneath the delicate lace of locust leaves
Standing in pure receptiveness.
The sequestered wake of passionless memories.

The startling crack of tree limbs
Under the bulldozer's steel
Tread, the retreat of nature
Bleeding fresh earth and poisoned springs,
The twining suckers of disease, the helpless
Wait, the brief words of the surgeon
And the opening made in the dream.
With sealing words to one so long a friend
And the sudden handclasp of manly vigor.
The exuberance and good times of gathered kin,
The plump hand of the baby weakly beating
And pressing my cheek.
The half-promise made to brown eyes
Patiently waiting, the words finding the mark
Well hidden in the foliage of myself.

FOURTEENTH ODE

How good it is when we strive together
And deal peacefully with one
Another in generous enlargements
Of our bounds and consciousness.
We shall use this life well
For why should we torture it?
It goes best with those who
Nourish it and observe its ways.
The days become an open
Art with us and strains
Of music can be heard in them.
Our varied skills are drawn
Each across the other and many works
Issue marvelously from these crossing
Bents as the rising of notes
From the rasp and vibrant
Crossings of bow and viol string.
Thus our passions and our
Acts are wrought to things of peace and use,
And rarely need we invoke the laws
Or split hairs between us.
There are some with hate who
Come among us

But their poison shall not keep.
Nor do the fanatics scorch our eyes.
The moistening of our
Bodies and a temperate breadth of vision
Give them protection.
In all these things we do not become
Nor wish to be, one.
We are each whole, being human
Instruments of varied and responsive
Voices, crooning and speaking our
Own bits and lines.
Often we pause and listen,
Hearing the voices of others, odd,
Arresting and moving.
Some sounding notes we
Have never heard, some
Gnarled and roughened,
Some piping shrill,
Some softly lilting,
Some seeming to take our part a while,
Each with his or her own
Strangeness bringing our
Senses to life.
We see that no apologies are needed,
That the earth bears many minds
And builds and colors in generous profusion.
We see that the differences and contrasts
Are enrichments of existence

And make life more than
A little trail.
We look about us, reaching beyond
Ourselves, and therein is a liberation.
Thus, resiliently trying and blending
The known and unknown,
Taking in the oddities and sting
And sweetness of others, our
Lives become larger than our own
And we discover the earth and feel it home.

II
A NEARNESS

THE NIGHT

The hour has come.
Let us take of the sweetness of the night
And in our light breathing
Thoughts and fresh remembrances
Glide free of the grasp of things.
Though hid away the ushering stars may be
Guessed in their steady glistering orbs.
Sounds that would disturb muffle up
And become lost from idling sense.
Neither breath nor heart is heard.
How good it is but to be
And let the slow sweep of the sea-bathed
World round and turn
As dusty day drifts off.
The soft lustrous light, sometimes seen
Harsh and crossed, melts
As the waxen glow of dusk roses.
The hour of our communion has come.
We enter the wondrous stream
Feeling the slightest tremor
As the current enfolds and cradles.
No word need be uttered,
The ecstasy wafts free.

Brushing silently over the lips
Unnamed wishes and hopes rise, turn
And sway majestically
As unknown flowers nod in murmuring air.
The crestless waves of the night's passing
Wake roll and curl and close about
Turning away the outer globe as velvet sheds
A waterdrop or a mote of quicksilver.
How freely life floods now,
Seeming here to amass its pools
And fill for all the flow.
We float at ease.
What comes will come, be a while
And go beyond again.
The tides hold distant sway and are welcome
For they work and tug with us.
The world is well enough that it holds
This sweet session when we may become composed
And ravel out our troubles with our delights
Our consummations and our hopes.
We do not come to ask nor to receive
But to approach and perchance to touch.
What passes in this gentle pervading
Existence cannot be seized
For it flows among us as the copious
Essence of our noblest and fullest selves.
Now all the great heaving mass must
Lay itself down and take a breath,

The heavy brute no less than
The exhausted one of delicate virtue.
Let us whisper in their ears
Encouragements and happy ways.
We are rich in them
And overflow of their abundance
But so many are poor in them
And dry and cracked within.
We shall give clear waters to them
For the waters of this love are better than wine
And go as balm upon the sores of the breast.
They will revive as drooping flowers
And turn all about and wonder whence it came.
How beautiful are the footprints of this night
Over the memory.
Time's measures dip and spill with succulent drops
Falling numberless through golden boughs.
The air of the night steals its gossamers,
It rises and falls as the breath of the lake
Wreathing and wisping the gentle isle,
Breathing over dull embers and temples.
Our presence interfuses and dissolves,
Effortlessly roiling and subliming.
Who are the transgressors among us, sleeping.
They have come far.
They may not be denied.
Rising up in the tender night
They reach, trembling, solemnly promising.

We shall not forget.
We bend over and catch up one
Then another faint.
Our arms and cheeks are comforting
With clumsy rude meaning.
They look up to us with thankful
And grateful brimmed eyes.
Come, gather strength and come with us.
Our way is longer but
It is more beautiful and happier.
We call to you softly. Surely you must hear.
Suddenly in the midst of an act
You stop and lay aside your things to listen.
Come, let us go together.
Do not fear. We shall be faithful.
One falling, another shall rise.
Always renewing, constantly and ceaselessly
Renewing and hesitantly unfolding.
Imperceptible transformations, slowly moving,
Soundlessly and wondrously receiving
The charge, the effuse,
Pouring forth marvelously.
Measured according to all times,
Not by these times alone,
And by the green futurities bearing
The fruit of us.
This hour is but a breath on the way,
The mute observance

Of the settling compass needle,
A sip at the spring,
A glance over the shoulder,
A few words with the strongest and surest,
Uttering hardly a sound.

AT THE PROMISED HOUR

At the promised hour
I hurry to you
Lying pale in the fevered storm.
We rise through all, my being
Wrapped about your trembling body,
My cool cheek pressed to yours hot.
Here, here I am,
It is my cheek with yours,
They are my eyes that shine for yours,
They are my hands that press for yours.
I shall keep with you
And succour you and comfort you,
And I shall stir up nourishment in your blood.

NOW UNTO MERCY

And I come in the flutter
Of the broken wing,
And in the scream of the torn
Soldier boy I come,
I vibrate in your memory.
I whisper in the curse of the drunkard
Awash in his wreckage,
And again I cry out
In the snarl of the cornered breadwinner,
He is frightened and I speak out of him.
Behold! I come in the snuffle
Of the smothering child,
In the anguish of the amputated lovers,
In the moan of the cancer host,
And in the still.
I come to be with you
And to rise up in your troubled thoughts.
Keep me always.

DESINENCE

It is ended.
Not all the wailing ever wrung,
Nor all the tears heavy salted
And swallowed, nor the fondled memories,
Nor all the wishes wished and rued
Down long stares of blankness
Can call it back.
Nor shall there end
The unguessed beginnings
Brought in the lap of the tides.

THE ONE COMPOSED

Cool and composed
I stand beside you,
I heard what you heard,
I see the trembling of your hand,
And I hear the trembling of your throat,
Yet I am cool and composed:
For there is something more to be heard,
Resting quiet in the memory.

FROM SLUMBERS AND DEPTHS

Some teach you lowliness
And helplessness and melancholy
And a deep crying
For what you cannot find,
Stirring a liquorous stew for suckle
When you are weak with hungers.
But these presences are not to cut
The sinews of your spirit
Nor break your will across another,
But to midwife gristle
And the gentlest power
Amid the heaves of pain and joys,
And to sing for your births and merge
In the wondrous river of life,
Tumbling, deep running and placidly pooling.
With lines and bits of these verses
They may be roused and brought up
From slumbers and depths where they lie
Part formed or forgot.
There is no need to strain eagerly,
The cradle of the deep rocks at will.
Nor be alarmed when something
Slips from your grasp and is lost
Or disappears to become part of the rest.

NOR EAGLE NOR LAMB

Often have you been
Admonished to be proud,
And many times admonished
To humbleness.
Now it is time to advance,
Not one nor the other will do.
Be neither proud nor humble,
Nor poison nor antidote,
Nor eagle nor lamb,
But you, unfolding and worthy.

THIS TO ANSWER

Must I shock you to make you listen?
Must I tell you unfathomable lies
To make you believe?
Must I crush your hopes
To make you tender?
Or do you recognize the signs
Of simple truths?
What I tell you has no fashion
And no deception,
It will wear well with you,
And it will bring you
Close to the vitals of your life.

THE FISHER

Here is my many-latticed net
So patiently woven and pliant.
Take it with you. And now and then,
As you study the sands,
Fling it wide away wheeling and skimming
The brined diamond-showering breeze.
What you take from the gurge and the crests
Will be live and whole
And dripping with their element.
Froth and seaweed and perhaps
Some curious pieces of dark
Dead wood may come with them,
But there will not be the deathly
Precision of the sharp pointing spear.

THE MIGHTY AND THE GENTLE

The gentle have powers to draw
The loves of peace into the mighty
As sweetly as sweet by tooth,
For they are wont to know them,
And even so are the mighty
Wont to have need for them
And be in their own peril for them.

THE OBSCURE

Come little ones,
Ah little ones
Who can hardly
Be caught by an eye,
Let us bake bricks
And knead mortar,
Each may bring a straw
Or some grains of sand
Or drops of water,
Some few may bring plumbs,
Then shall we build
With grains and drops,
In the shade
And happily.

HONEYCOMB

Her slender silver face
Lives in moon-stillness.
She gazes long,
Hungers some,
Partakes modestly,
Listens, chuckles, ponders,
Storing and delving a honeycomb of life
Beneath a pale tranquil surface.
Some say laugh, enjoy yourself, be like us.
Another says don't laugh, enjoy yourself,
Be like you.

SOLITUDE

The lonely are not the alone
But they who wake not to solitude,
For solitude is the dark
Or yet the light
Spilling out of acts and creations
Done for perfect eyes,
And the flawed eyes of earthlings
Among their climes and clouds.

AS STRANGE MUSIC

The beauty of a homely face is withheld
As strange music.
Sensed in the waft and drift of a moment
It wheels and vanishes in the wilderness
To peep from haunts of pools and crags.
Sometimes gliding from shade to shade
Whisping by the memory,
Sometimes rambling off lost and wild
Down swirling mists to fall
Without a sound,
Sometimes startling, rushing out
From hollows and folds to leap
Naked on the open plain—
And in that instant crushed by light.
And sometimes remaining near
Wrapped in so little as a smile or air.

LEAVE

Will you stay with me a while,
Then I'll go.
We'll walk a ways and talk
And say things we never say.
And we'll listen to the clattered
Sighing of the streets
And the distant horn
And wish we could go on.
Then we'll sit down
But I'll not tell you how it was.
We will look away
And see what we always see
In the way of strangers.
I will tell you who I am,
You'll not know but does it matter.
Then we'll swallow our crusts and feel time
Stumble and wait.
You will think me gentle
But will not know.

THE TREE

Standing alone under the bare fists
Of the weathers, baked with heats,
Dried with drouths, coddled with dews,
Chilled and cracked of branches
And all shrieked upon
By the meanest winds,
The tree stands and gives.
With time the fair returns
And the tree sends forth
Its tender hopes and bines,
The good season is kind to them
And bathes them and warms and feeds them,
There peacefully waving on the gentle airs
The young greens weave out their life
To a plan of simple needs.
Then returns the time
When the sun becomes distant,
The voices of nature crack
And lose their warble,
And the sky is torn
And whipped over crusted earth,
Again the tree is shaken
And rawly tried from limb to root

By lashing bitter winds.
They blast upon its heart
And wrestle it and twist its limbs.
But the tree has a suppleness,
It plys the wind
Like a great vein of fire.

SPOKEN FOR A CHILD

Teach me the letters
That I may see
Beyond my sight,
Teach me the hand
That I may speak
Beyond my voice,
But engraft in me
Deep, half as deep
As your love,
A discipline of self,
That I may not be
Tormented by myself,
That I may go safely
Through vinegar seas and sweet syrups.

THE CRAB

See, the crab!
How gnarled and strangely formed.
Feel the hard shell
And the intricate designs.
Such sensitive feelers.
He is testy and shy.
Come, he will bite you,
Or more gladly skitter away.
But wait.
Perhaps he is the most interesting one of all.

LOCKLESS

Lay up a wealth of riches within your brows,
Then may they be close to hand
And sure to keep,
Such a chest is not hid in the dark
Nor made heavy and ponderous,
Jauntily it carries your fortune
Among glitter or ruin
Among power and crush
Through shallows, black forests
And thieves' hollows.
A treasure box never lost.

MEANS AND ENDS

There is the talk of the means
And the talk of the ends,
That the means are all
And the ends are all.
Yet how can means fulfill
If they point to vacant ends.
And how are ends human ends
If the means want automatic people.
And again do not means beget ends
No less than ends beget means,
For means are as well
The beginnings of ends.
Nor is it summed in the balance
Of weighty matters.
For surely the time of life
Is spun out with means
Seeming to lack a heft of ends.
And how often is some mountainous
Coil of tangled means
Light in balance with a faltered breath.
What of a song?
It is weightless, yet it fills
And rises with meaning

Being many times means and end in one.
Thus the making of life
Is with the means and the ends,
Wound and woven each with each,
As the vine entwines and weaves its being
With moist root and curling tendril
The podding bloom within
And the tipmost bloom and reach.

A COUNTRY WALK

Moving into simplicities
With careless tosses,
Hearing not small doubts or questions,
Feeling the melt of vibrations into waves,
The soft air falling and folding
Over hands and face,
The earth firm and trustworthy under foot,
The gentle downs basking and rolling,
The flawless spears
Of grass lithely swaying,
The great tree weaving and gliding,
The water sounds of the leaves
Swishing and rustling.
The gurgle and bound ahead
Of the pebble,
The leathered toe pressing the pebble
Flush into the moist earth,
The completion and fulfillment
Coming out of this simple perfect act.
The dibbling in the moss-banked
Run of the water,
The flow of thoughts
Into the waters and juices of the earth,

The bobbing about and cleansing of them,
And the floating away
In wondrous curling eddies.
An embedded mirroring crystal
Flares and dims.
Slowly and ponderously, invisible
Silent churnings roll up the puffs
And veils of the heavens.
The last rimple vanishes with the whisps.
An inner balance is almost heard.

REPOSE

My hands are folded
And my brow is light,
And I lie in the
Lap of content,
For this day
I have believed
What I have done,
And now is the sweet night that follows.

III
THE HOUSE OF THE BELOVED

CANTO ONE

Seek you the pillar of security
In your house?
Seek you the lock of security
In your labour?
Seek you the embrace of security
In your beloved?
See you the sinews of it in meat,
And the everlasting thread in cloth?
Seek you stronghold but in these?
Then you delude yourself and cheat yourself.
For it is as much made within you
And of you, and of what you take into your spirit.

CANTO TWO

Each may dedicate a part of himself
And that part shall be priceless.
If he gives with labour
He may give his labour
If he gives with talent
He may give his talent
If he be vigilant he may give his vigil,
So also with the lightning
And sweat of his brains.
And beyond such things
Beyond the common tasks or the dearest blood
Something more shall be given—
Full and overflowing.
Neither drouth nor spring nor
Sand grits shall dry it up,
Nor good fortune nor ill nor ease,
It shall be as the deepest well.
Whosoever gives in this kind ascends,
Even if those who stand near him fail him.

CANTO THREE

Beautifully simple and yet astounding,
Richly modest,
And yet so fearlessly free,
Genitor of trust, bone of character,
Such is honesty.
This plain yet glinting quality brings
A vigor and purity among us,
Moving and staying many things
To keep open the ways.
Appearing boldly or in most
Gentle voice it speaks a certain
Native tongue long bred
In the heart and reason of man.
For it is that all beings at once or at last
Draw to the clean one,
And though they know it not
They give him praise even as
They speak of distant things.
And this he feels though he hear it not,
Sensing it in the light of life, in the life
Loved, in life enduring.

CANTO FOUR

Not the grief of the deep sunken heart
Nor the wild grief of flesh torn out
Nor the tired grief of the ages
But each is by a way
Where grief cannot follow,
And the grieved cry
Out and ache for it aloud
And are swallowed up again
For they know not where it is.
Cry no more, grieving one,
Hide away no more,
It lives all about you now,
At your hand
And by your side.

CANTO FIVE

That you may be saved from crushing
Your breast, give.
That you may be rich in spirit, give.
Give of what you would take,
Give of what you cry out for,
And know of giving in anguish.
With gentleness, destroy the fear
Of an iron world.
But give wisely, give not whatsoever
Is asked, there are parasites many
And many that are weak.
And soften not another's mettle
That you may gain the pleasure of giving,
Have vision in your largess.
Give brightly—not darkly,
And give out of the lode of yourself,
For if you give only of alms,
If you give only of money,
If you give only of things,
What have you given?
What if a man draw out
A hair from his head and give it?
But what if he draw out

A piece of himself and give this?
Take joy in the sacrifice.
The pruned tree of fruit is most healthy,
And so the fruit created.
Give creatively,
And you shall have meaning.
How find you then singing to yourself?
I have done this thing that I did love to do.

CANTO SIX

Even as the gentle night enfolds
The dropped calf so shall I bring sweet sleep
To thee. In a mantle of tenderness I bring thee
Sleep and blow out the fires in thine eyes.
Moving in the forest of thy thoughts
Among the leafy hopes and murmurous
Springs, in the dimming light of thine eyes,
Enshaded there, patiently holding
The slackening line, I slip the knots,
Letting fall lavish coils in the slumbrous air.
Peace for thy heart and thy tousled
Forehead I bring, with merciful quiet
Fresh liniments and forgetfulness.
Though you did lose me in the day
Yet have I returned to you faithfully.
Lo, I hang dewy crystals upon
Thy eyelids and touch thy cheeks
With soft sighs of myrrh.
The gardens of Jaipur are so bedded and tended,
Even as the flow of the Afton this peacefullness.
Come, steep thy limbs in ease
And blessed heaviness. Droop thy head upon thy
Bed and I will pour soft hours over thee,

Making a bath of sweet humors and dissolving
Thoughts to lap about thy slumbers.
Take the fold of the dreamy cloak.
Come, be hushed with kindness.
The blue mountains of sleep are
Sinking with their lovely power.
Soon the gleaming clasp melts
And then at last in cool sleep
Thou shalt leave me, yet I not thee.

CANTO SEVEN

Suffer no man to lose faith in himself,
For he that is bereft of faith
In himself has a wretched sickness,
His guts hang loose in him
And he mortifies
And sinks down.
Honor the cowards, the thieves
And the felons and all the broken
That gather themselves up and bear
The new faith in themselves,
For they may be transformed.

CANTO EIGHT

Then at certain times
Go from friends
And walk among the sunken
The anguished and the poor,
Seek them to rub against you
And to soil your manners,
Talk against none
Nor think against any of them,
But take their part inwardly
Reaching into their sorrows
And their lacks.
Then go, and remember them,
And keep a part of them.

CANTO NINE

They are magnificent
Who suffer great pain in silence.
Behold how they under their tortures
Purchase the peace of others,
Neither crying out
Nor breaking before them,
Giving way never complete.
Opening their locked up silences
Only to release the springs and stretch
Out the coils for a stronger winding.
Taking the very power
Of pain itself to tame it,
Seizing the shreds
Of anguish and making them
To a binding cord.
In this proving strength, in this
Proving humanity,
In this proving love.
Though they groan under their breath
Yet they possess a serenity untouchable.
Knowing there is a bond between
Them and all who suffer,
Knowing at the moment

Of supreme pain there are
Those who suffer more,
Knowing they also
Can endure still more.
Though they lie helpless they are mighty.

CANTO TEN

You see yourself as a failure,
As one fallen and broken.
But you have forgotten,
You have forgotten you are
A being of many modest successes
Proving you, and only now this
That engulfs and overwhelms you.
There is something of you
You cannot see,
Something both calming
And startling.
Perhaps you sometimes sense
Its presence though you cannot
Imagine its form or substance,
At moments unsuspected
It enters your actions
Powerful and penetrating,
Creating dominations and energies,
This without setting a ripple
In your memory.
It is always with you,
It is with you even now,
Be confident. Let it advance.

CANTO ELEVEN

The life is spent with desires—
Only moments with achievements.
Thus life's puddings are plummed
Baked and downed. And it is good,
For so is life never finished.
Yet some among these desires
Are ravenous and charged
With a raw and sweeping wildness.
And some among them
Hover ceaselessly about the ways
And crossings of frustration,
Swaying there and dangling
Like candy-coated wasps.
Yet, though they delight to carry off
The earth beneath your feet
Disdain to run with fears,
For it is when overshadowed
Or passed with quiet reason they
Drowsy droop and fall.
Nor look to the ways of life
Made to take out all desires,
There is no life human without
The workings of desire,

From the very stings and barbs
Spring fresh awakenings,
And the bees bear fertile
Pollens with their lancets.
There are some desires all golden
And molten-crystalled as honey,
They feed countless told
And untold satisfactions
Along their flow through life,
Among disharmonious conflicts
They come as a melody,
And the shrills and discords merge with
Them and become eased to lesser parts.
And there are great desires
Like huge slow-flighted birds that rise
Majestically in atmospheres removed
And far off from lower worlds
Yet wholly real and earthly-eyed,
Their days are many and long
And they sail the most full-sunned light,
And they in seeing most see lesser
Things as folds across the rolling spread.

CANTO TWELVE

The rock is made soft,
The water hardened,
The sheep is swallowed
And made to a finger,
And the ship got into a bottle.
So all things may be made
Unto the purpose,
The boldness and the gentleness,
The heard and the unheard,
The sleep and the wake,
The keen and the dull.
The offense, the chastisement,
The struggle, the acquiescence,
The wealth, and the want,
The clarities and the mysteries,
The song and the silence.
The beat of the heart
And the rest of the heart,
The love and the aversion,
The time of the rising up
And the time of the falling,
The tension, the ease,
The flaw and the perfection,
And the plunge and the wait;
The moment and the life.

CANTO THIRTEEN

Not as a locketed still likeness,
Nor slave in tender duty bonds,
Nor as a caged bird shrunken
And waiting hold the young one.
But high perched
On the raised up arm,
That it may go as a messenger
And a piece of the heart
Full and free sent out.
Crush it no more,
The young breast sucks and aches
For the tasting of the world winds
And the spew of burnt breath
Out the curious nostrils.
See how the wheeling world
Sweeps up this breath and essence
In its mantle, drawing it out
Even to fine indivisible faces,
Making it new mates and new work
And travels under the alloying
Light of gold and silver orbs,
And some full round again and home.

CANTO FOURTEEN

Keep peace with him you call enemy,
Talk with him and find his heart.
He is hid there in the darkness,
In the murmuring and the pounding,
In the closing and the squeezing
And the trembling and the hardening.
If his heart be a fearful heart
Give it all ease of reason,
If it be a blind grey muscle
That knows nothing but
Work and will
Draw it out of itself
And make of it something more,
If it be shrunken and away
Feed it and avail it,
If it be greedy
And did never grow satisfied with
Infancy's sweet plunders, then
Bear a sweet tooth and go weaning.
But if his heart be hid
In the shadow of your light
What of your light
And the reflections of it.

The pulse of him, the core
The chambered psyche,
They are there in their own
Strains and songs.
Search then, find the Rosettas
And keep peace with him.
For if you war upon him
And conquer him then must you
Make peace with him in misery.
Man cannot have comfort
In his heart without peace,
Nor can he have peace
And give oppression,
For oppression will find
The heart and haunt it
And grow sores there.
Though the oppressor fill himself
With huge philosophies
And great stores of reasons
Still the festering in him is fed
By the best in him and borne up
In his gorge by his loved ones,
And there is no peace in him
Till he give up and make it decent.
Though he twist and turn
And wallow his body in busy things,
Though he hide his mind
In convolutions and pleasures,

Still there comes a cry through it.
In the mirror comes
The face of the stranger,
And in the little children
Waits the face of the humbled.

CANTO FIFTEEN

May the white of thy rightness tumble
Gentle folds down among the green,
That righteousness be
Not a sterile thing upon thee
And whosoever strays before thy way.
Rise up, yea, rise up with rightness
Yet not so high as to pass over
In fumes and storms, breaking
Lightning bolts on them that totter,
Or in chill chinkless armour
White lipped and horsed on pride.
Let not the color and juice be
Squeezed out of thee,
The press of life makes wine
And the attire of life
Is but fleeting white
And soon stained by the purest tot.

CANTO SIXTEEN

As you love your little ones
So love one another.
Not alone the lambs and kittens
And sugar plums,
But the eagles and the turtles
And the magpies that scratch about.
When the sweet-faced and the dimpling
Darlings mew for notes of love
They receive them.
But the bold, the heavy-treading
The cool-skilled and the sharp-taloned
How often they are born to no soft mew
And taste no suppling milk
And are chill for it.
This love is not given for safekeep
But to be lost and swallowed up
And made part of the other.
A few sips, a little cup, even if
But a drop is spared,
It has a melting touch
And the sweet nourishments
Of a honeyed milk.
Then why spared

Or metered out or weighed?
Is this the dividing of a last flask?
Why it is more as the spilling of a spring
And the working of an udder that prospers
And burgeons with use.
For loving makes love.

Who gives abroad this gentle juice
Becomes richer of it and made full.
Though cuts may stain or deepen hues
What can dam a flowing love that has
A hundred teats and ways to flow.
As a fertile summer rain
It falls and runs all about
Even upon the butted roots,
Making them to glide among the stones.
And winters are not bare but fruitful
And burnished with a summer gold.

CANTO SEVENTEEN

Thy song shall touch me for I am
Thy high spirit and about thee always.
My raiment is of music and out of music
And deliverance my hand is stretched forth.
And it comes again like the sound
Of a voice born of the green mountains,
As the fresh brook that goes down to the prairie
Flooding forth over dry land with
The rippled strength of a youth's arm.
I charge thee not in fear
But in kindness. I shall not shake fright
Before thee for I lead thee away from travail.
What fury have I that am for thee?
I that am carried as the scent of flowers.
And I speak of life not of fantasy, therefore
Reality and plainness cannot destroy me
For I am with reality and plainness.
The world is not cheap and the neverland
A marvel, it is the neverland that is cheap
And builded with words, and the living reality is
Here at our hand and can be made
Good and of full happy hours.
Nor do I ignore the urge and purpose

Of the flesh but give light and life to it.
I am out of thee and thy brothers,
Not out of eternity, and therefore am not sterile.
I take thee through pain and through the bright
Streets of joy and laughter
Never to abandon thee in a ditch of penance.
When you run into the ditch how long should be
Wallow and woe? I am a lifter for thee
And float as a white cloud rich in the sun.
And I have as much truth in the light
As in the dark for my coverlet is like snow
To keep thee clean and warm, not to keep thee
In darkness and apart from men and women.
I shall show thee home among every kind
For I care for all nations and races,
And for the white, the black, the brown
And the beautiful shifting shades and the pink
Youth and grey age for they are all
Brothers and sisters one to another.
Therefore do I abhor hate and bigotry.
When brothers and sisters tear one
Another they are less than wild beasts
And the fowl of the barnyard.
In the power of justice I move among men
And yet I sweep the ground when the truth
Lies there, even when it lies with confusion
And foulness. I shall spit into the dust
That is ground by the cruel heel and make it

A mud to splatter and stick to him,
And I shall be like a changing pestilence to him
That he cannot find my arms.
I shall turn again and again
To make peacefulness and goodness prevail.
Then again I am like a loving father.
The eyes of my head are set in kindness
And my arm and my scapula are formed of courage.
Love is the blood of my veins.
When you fall into the well
Of loneliness reach for my hand
And I shall draw thee up.
Come to me when you are troubled
And I shall comfort thee.
Come to me when you are struck down
And I will give thee strength.
Come to me when you are joyous
And I will take nourishment from thee
And multiply thy quality.
The wind scatters the good seed with abandon
And the machine scatters the seed with precision
But I ruffle thee and plant thee lovingly
For I would keep thee from becoming
A machine of dead life.
I nourish the womb and semen
Of thy goodness, and every good thing you do
And every happy thing you do gives me
Food and drink. Yet when thine eyes

Would fix my body the probe passes
Through me clean like a sun ray in the water cup.
Still am I there as the drink for life
To make thee an enjoyer of life
Not merely an enjoyer of the exalted.
Drink deep and listen
How the music weaves lovely cloth and strong.
The wanderer of the night looks
To the stars that come up in his eyes
And drinks of them, and his feet are well placed.

CANTO EIGHTEEN

As you would others should do unto you
Do you even so unto them.
Keep this rich extract
Of justice with you
As in ten thousand tender vials
That one by one crush by
The press of day and turn of night,
Spilling and seeping silently into
Your thoughts, intermixing and working
And at last coming forth in ply
And course as naturally as breath.
Though many small injustices are
With this great justice yet so it is
With all the ways of man.
Therefore to the unjust turn
And give justice even as you would
Give straightness to a twisted limb.
And to the harsh give mildness,
And to the cold and hid
Give warmth, and to the false truth.
This is the beginning of things among us.

CANTO NINETEEN

Through the rounds and whets
Of time it comes that they who
Would slash the sky abrade themselves
And sharpen the edge of fate.
But they who go patiently do most.
The listener hears the inner music
And he sways to it
And his time prospers.
For the mansion of life is heaped
And builded up from moments turns
And morrows one to another
All laced with fickle greens
Springing and fading in single
Days and little uneven windowed
Stairs winding up the future.
While happiness moves among
The cool and hyaline columns of hours
Barely noticed, as though
It were engaged forever.

CANTO TWENTY

Some go forth and do a great work,
Let them have the praise for it.
And some do excellent
Works, let them have their praise.
And some do beautiful and good
Things, surely they are due no less.
Yet the most of what is good
Is plain and is done in the letterless
Days and not proclaimed Here is it.
And so is the praise plain
Or croaked out in bits or not at all.
Or threading a mute trail
Through afterdays, long forgotten
And half formed to other fates
It suddenly pulls in the moistening
Grip of a babe,
Or loosed and shaken from mortal
Lease it tides in shining airs.
Then sing to the day
To this day in its own,
As it rises and approaches so
Surely with invisible undulous steps,
As it brushes your cheek, as it

Quietly fills and lingers perhaps
Holding out no more than
A pebble or veil,
With largeness and ease of heart sing,
Freely and trusting sing and sing on,
Sing to this day this common day.
The day will not be silent to you.

Index of First Lines

A NOTE ON THE TYPE

This book is set on the linotype in Caslon, a Dutch-English style typeface named for William Caslon (1692-1766), the first great English typefounder. Between 1720 and 1726 Caslon developed his typefaces, basing them on the prevailing Dutch style, derived through Van Dijck, Jannon and Garamond from Aldine roman.

Composed, printed, and bound by
The Haddon Craftsmen, Scranton, Pennsylvania